Sesame Street® Self-Care

Big Feelings

Learn Healthy Ways to Manage Emotions with Sesame Street

Whitney Sanderson

Lerner Publications ◆ Minneapolis

In this series, young readers will learn different ways they can take care of themselves! Come along as Elmo and his *Sesame Street* friends explore how healthy habits—like eating well and expressing your feelings—help you grow smarter, stronger, and kinder.

Sincerely,
the Editors at Sesame Workshop

Table of Contents

Many Feelings

There are so many feelings. Happy, sad, frustrated, excited, disappointed, and angry are just some of them.

I feel excited today!

Manage Your Feelings

We all have big feelings, and all feelings are important.

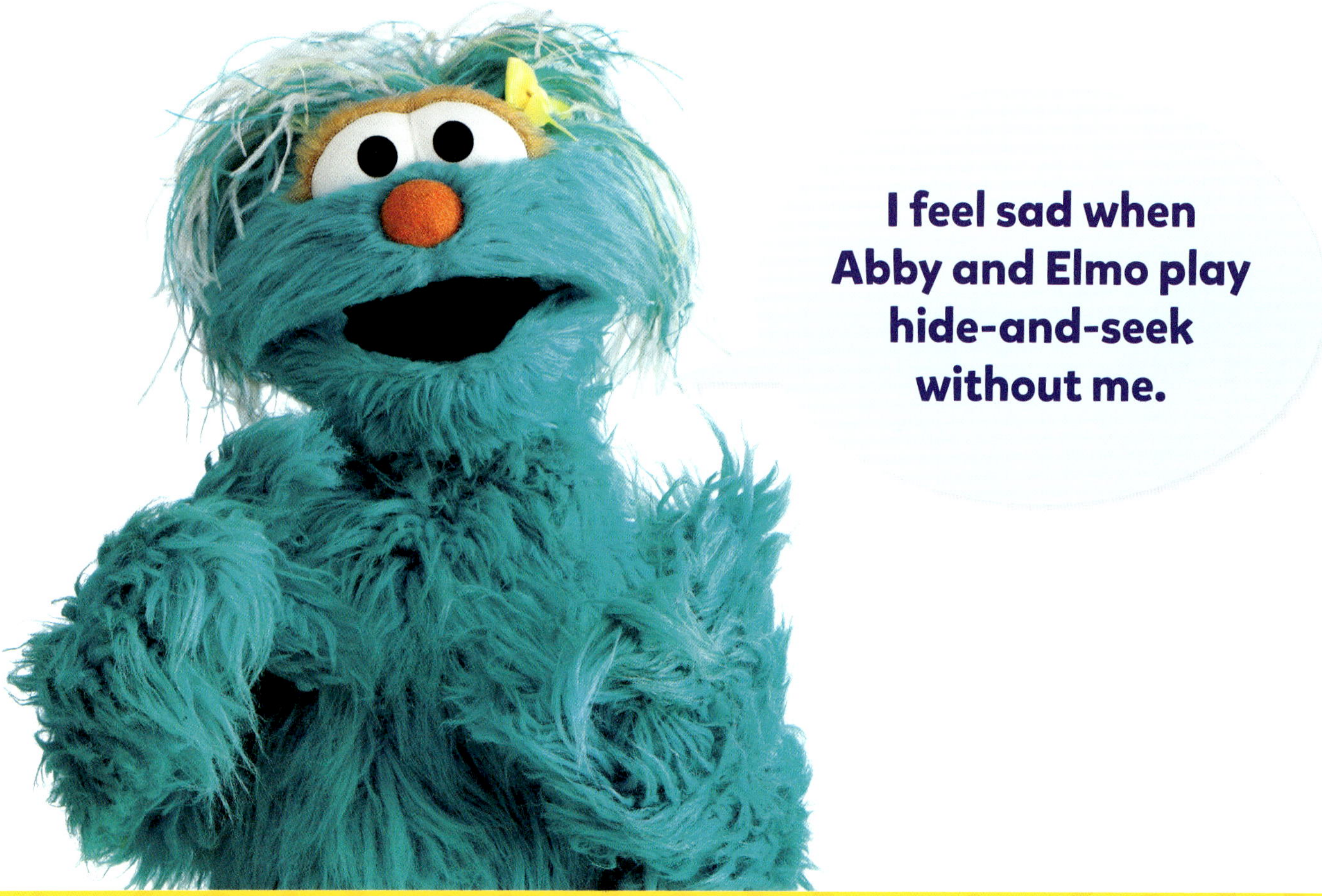

Noticing how we're feeling helps us understand why we feel that way.

When you're having a big feeling, pause and say these phrases to yourself:

"I notice . . ." —How is your body feeling?

"I feel . . ." —Name the feeling you are feeling.

"I can . . ." —What is something you can do to help your body feel calmer and help you feel better?

I notice that my face is hot.
I feel frustrated because my block tower fell down!
I can take a deep breath and try again.

If you're feeling angry, you can shake a glitter jar. The glitter is like the feelings swirling around inside you. While you watch the glitter settle, take a slow, deep breath.

I love watching the glitter. It looks magical and helps my body feel calmer.

If you feel excited, you can move your body. You can dance and wiggle your arms and legs!

If you're feeling sad, sometimes it helps to get or give a hug.

Giving Tango a hug makes Elmo feel better.

I'm disappointed I lost the game of checkers, Bert.
How about we take a lion breath, Ernie?

If you're feeling disappointed, try taking a lion breath. Take a slow, deep breath in through your nose, and roar as you slowly breathe out.

You can try hand-on-heart breathing when you're feeling nervous. Put your hand over your heart. Then take a slow, deep breath in through your nose, and slowly breathe out through your mouth.

Sometimes I feel scared to play my guitar in front of people. I put my hand over my heart and take deep breaths.

We can do lots of things to help us when we have a big feeling. We can notice how our body is feeling, name our feeling, and do something to help our body feel calmer.

Healthy You!

There are many ways to help your mind and body feel calmer. Lion breaths and glitter jars are two examples. You can also try butterfly breathing. Hold your arms out, and imagine they are butterfly wings. Take a slow, deep breath in and lift your wings up. Then slowly breathe out and float your wings back down.

Glossary

checkers: a game played on a checkerboard by two people

disappointed: a feeling you have when something doesn't happen the way you wanted it to

frustrated: a feeling you have when you try to do something but can't

glitter: tiny bits of shiny material for arts and crafts

Read More

Hughes, Sloane. *Don't Sweat It: How to Navigate Big Emotions.* Minneapolis: Bearport, 2022.

Miller, Marie-Therese. *How Are You Feeling? Naming Your Emotions with Sesame Street.* Minneapolis: Lerner Publications, 2023.

Rummel, Lynn. *I Remember My Breath: Mindful Breathing for All My Feelings.* Huntington Beach, CA: Free Spirit, 2023.

Photo Acknowledgments

Image credits: MStudioImages/Getty Images, p. 4; maroke/Getty Images, p. 7; ciricvelibor/Getty Images, p. 8; Vladimir Prusakov/Shutterstock, p. 9 (blocks); pixdeluxe/Getty Images, p. 10; seksan Mongkhonkhamsao/Getty Images, p. 13; vandervelden/Getty Images, p. 14; Liudmila Chernetska/Getty Images, p. 16; fizkes/Getty Images, p. 18; Deepak Sethi/Getty Images, p. 20.

Design element: Dedraw Studio/Shutterstock.

Index

For Faisal

Lerner Publications Company
An imprint of Lerner Publishing Group, Inc.
241 First Avenue North
Minneapolis, MN 55401 USA

For reading levels and more information, look up this title at www.lernerbooks.com.

Main body text set in Mikado. Typeface provided by HVD.

Editor: Annie Zheng **Designer:** Laura Otto Rinne

Library of Congress Cataloging-in-Publication Data

Names: Sanderson, Whitney, author.
Title: Big feelings : learn healthy ways to manage emotions with Sesame Street ® / Whitney Sanderson.
Description: Minneapolis, MN : Lerner Publications , [2025] | Series: Sesame street self-care | Includes bibliographical references and index. | Audience: Ages 4–8 | Audience: Grades K–1 | Summary: "We all have big feelings, and understanding why they happen and how to manage them is important. From moving it out to breathing techniques, young readers learn ways to help manage their emotions"– Provided by publisher.
Identifiers: LCCN 2024006365 (print) | LCCN 2024006366 (ebook) | ISBN 9798765643716 (library binding) | ISBN 9798765657959 (epub)
Subjects: LCSH: Emotions—Juvenile literature.
Classification: LCC BF723.E6 S29 2025 (print) | LCC BF723.E6 (ebook) | DDC 155.4/124–dc23/eng/20240514

LC record available at https://lccn.loc.gov/2024006365
LC ebook record available at https://lccn.loc.gov/2024006366

ISBN 979-8-7656-6241-0 (pbk.)

Manufactured in the United States of America
1-1010920-52412-7/12/2024